STATES OF HAPPINESS

Suzanne Batty published her debut pamphlet *Shrink* (1997) with smith|doorstop books, and two book-length collections with Bloodaxe, *The Barking Thing* (2007) and *States of Happiness* (2018). She won the Poetry Society's Anne Born Prize in its inaugural year, 2015.

She studied for an MA in Creative Writing at Sheffield Hallam University and subsequently became a lecturer there. She has collaborated with musicians, visual artists, photographers and printmakers, and uses creative writing to support people experiencing and recovering from mental distress. She also writes short fiction and for the theatre. She lives in Manchester where she was a founder member of urban poetry project the A6 Poets.

SUZANNE BATTY

States of Happiness

BLOODAXE BOOKS

Copyright © Suzanne Batty 2018

ISBN: 978 1 78037 426 0

First published 2018 by
Bloodaxe Books Ltd,
Eastburn,
South Park,
Hexham,
Northumberland NE46 1BS.

www.bloodaxebooks.com
For further information about Bloodaxe titles
please visit our website or write to
the above address for a catalogue.

Cover design: Neil Astley & Pamela Robertson-Pearce.

Printed in Great Britain by Bell & Bain Limited, Glasgow, Scotland, on
acid-free paper sourced from mills with FSC chain of custody certification.

This is for my family, present and absent, with love

ACKNOWLEDGEMENTS

Some poems in this collection have previously appeared in *Poetry Review*, *Poetry News* and *Dreamcatcher*. 'Grandmother' appeared in the Raving Beauties anthology *Hallelujah for 50ft Women* (Bloodaxe Books, 2015). 'Dreams of Warthogs' was previously published in *Shrink* (smith | doorstop books, 1998) and was reprinted in *Thirty at Thirty* (smith | doorstop books, 2016). 'Horse Therapy' won the Café Writers Open Poetry Competition 2016. 'Severe Weather Warning' won the York Prize 2016. 'Our Birthday' won second prize in the Philip Larkin and East Riding Poetry Competition 2013. 'Wincobank' won second prize in the Nottingham Open Poetry Competition 2013. 'Jesus on a train from Mumbai' was longlisted for the Montreal International Poetry Competition 2013.

'Gay-Lyfe Pets and Aquatics' was commissioned by Manchester Literature Festival and local radio station All FM in 2011. The poems in *Angels of Anarchy* were commissioned by Manchester Literature Festival and Manchester Art Gallery as a response to the exhibition of women surrealist artists in 2009. 'The Nameless Tree', 'Severe Weather Warning', 'Conversation at Cricieth Castle' and 'The Raft' were originally part of a "poetry conversation" with Milorad Krystan-ovitch, commissioned by Like Starlings online poetry project (2009).

'William Bradford, Elder' was one of the winning poems in the *Poetry News* members competition and went on to win the inaugural Anne Born Prize in 2013. This gave me the opportunity to be mentored by Penelope Shuttle whilst working on this collection – thank you Penny for your clear and compassionate eye and for your absolute belief in these poems.

Thanks to my dear friends especially Mark, Cal, Jan and Helen for making happiness seem possible again. Mark, without your unwavering love and impeccable judgement this book could not have been written.

Thank you, Joan, Rachel and Catriona – always, always above and beyond...

I'm grateful to Neil Astley for his patience and understanding.

Finally, thanks to Roxie, the blue dog – more rescuer than rescued.

CONTENTS

My twin, the fearless

in memory of Nicola

Breech

Somewhere ahead of me goes my twin sister –
we're cramped like specimens, she wants to be free.
She pushes her little creased feet against me
speeds herself from our crimson-weeded pool.
I want to catch her ankle and make her stay –
all around me, anemones raise their voices
calling to her *do not go forward*.

My twin is determined, her mouth a drawn line.
I see the strength of her clenched fists, the spiky blackness
of her hair. She pushes her head forwards, her chin lifted,
swims out in a rush of seaweed, out into dry antiseptic air.

I can't follow her. My feet are where my head should be –
I'm a rock jammed between boulders, unable to move.
No longer the length of my flesh against hers, no more
our hearts hinged together; never again the two of us
sliding around the sloping genius of the womb.

The Dewerstone

At the foot of the rock, between crooked branches,
my father is hungry. He has been on the moor all day,
searching for the hard fact of an ammunition tin.
In among the furze and fern, my mother hangs out endless white
        nappies
like prayer flags. She'll bind all our wounds with creeping plants,
collect balls of moss like green dormice to cram in our mouths.
She always has her hands full, carries us, twin 1 and twin 2,
like clots of mud. When we climb to the top, my big sister
carries a bottle of turpentine, four paper cups –
my mother has shown her how to fill them up.

At the summit ravens fall through poisonous air,
skewered by a buzzard's scream. My mother asks us
to hold her wrists so she can't strike stone with her raw
twin-tubbed fists. She closes her eyes, describes the view –
the Eddystone lighthouse, a charcoal burner's hut,
on snowy days a cloven footprint. Taking her lipstick
we paint her red, spit on mascara, darken her lashes.

What has happened to my father? He's walked ten miles
to the butcher's, who hands him a carrier bag
of dubious accounts, another which he fills with slabs of pale tripe –
my mother will cook both in milk from a cow
whose body's wrapped round with black mourning.

Our birthday

Eight years old, we have come to the mine workings to play;
cards on the caravan mantelpiece, new elastic for our knee-high
white socks. The September sky is wide open. Under our red sandals
earth is ochre, burnt umber, ultramarine. My father, standing,
holds my twin's hand and my hand. My mother in black clothes
cuts up her saffron cake. We can hear the mine creaking, the flatness
of the sea; my father's nervous beauty. We have dressed our dolls
in matching clothes, poured gin carefully into their holey mouths.

My father ties our dog to a tree on boggy ground. He says:
the grass is gold the trees are gold the smoke from the huts
is sheep's wool caught on a fence we are sheep's wool caught
on a fence; he has a low voice like a cow's. When he carries us both
on his shirtless back, my twin cries: can't you smell the cricket stumps,
the sunburn, the muscle? But I think: will she set fires under
the caravan and lock me inside? She promised we would run around
with stale bread and forget-me-nots, but that was before.
After that, everything happened.

My twin, the fearless

Up in the cherry tree, high in its taut red arms,
I'm rubbing my fingers over gashed bark,
soothing its wounds with my hands.
My twin and I are like peg dolls in a toy garden;
we're wearing our blue dress and our red dress.

I'm picking blossom, stripping the tree like a locust,
my twin on the ground like a faraway bird.
I want her to climb up but she throws me
a snake's glare; she will not speak.

The truth is she has fallen, she is always falling;
neither earth nor tree can balance her –
maybe she's too sharp-pretty, too cunning. Maybe
it's her lop-sided pigtails, her uneven hem.

Our dog, in a green sunhat, pushes its nose
into her ribs, wagging its amputated tail. It licks
the little skulls of her knees, will not let the doll-doctors
touch her; they are masked and naked, waving their plastic
stethoscopes. They draw words from their mouths
like a never-ending tongue; the word that stays with me is
crippled –
it penetrates my skin.

Huddled in our bunk beds later,
the rumble of my father's voice climbs up
the stairs. He's a matador, glittering and helpless,
silently chewing the stained stalk of his pipe.
I won't leave you, not ever, I whisper to my twin,
but she's rigid, not listening, facing the wall.

Eight years later, I'm on the hard shoulder, the sun rising.
My heart's a butchered slab in a plastic bag.
With my head shaven, I don't care what happens to me.
I hold up my thumb and my hand-painted sign,
mouth at the wave of traffic, please. *Please*.

Curtains

There were these yellow tartan curtains;
I remember the hard thick weight of them.
When my twin and I wrapped ourselves up,
I would cover my face, the tartan tight against
my open mouth, gladly suffocating for her.
Then she could have my yellow rubber bear –
you could rip bits out of it with your teeth.

When my mother came home, my twin would trot
across the carpet to be lifted up, one shoe missing,
a sign of her red innocence. I would kick the doors
and furniture until my big sister grabbed me by my tartan
dress, whispered *children with sparse hair don't eat.*

I knew they didn't mean it. I knew by their certain blue eyes
and their softly clenched fists that they loved me.

Dartmoor

Driving rain. The three of us run across the moor,
snagging our ankles in the heather. Eyes closed,
arms braced, we plunge into the gorse. Above us,
non-specific Germans fly their ghost planes in and out of the mist;
we must throw ourselves down like a crime scene.

The grown-ups don't know about terror.
They're huddled together on the path; we know
they hate us for carrying things – their disembodied eyes,
their recalcitrant genes.

Migraine

What we hope for is a man like our father
although he lies in a darkened room, a mask
across his eyes, piles of foreign coins on the dresser –

we have to tiptoe past like accidentally unborn children.
My twin thinks the room is full of bird's bones and elves
making shoes on the anvil of our father's head. She

knows the dust devils underneath his bed, she has
been there, polishing the bedsprings, tying ribbons. I
have pushed open the door and blinked in the afternoon

gloom, heard her hissing at me – *mine mine mine*. She
throws her tongue out at me; it's curled up at the edges,
in its valley, a toothpick she will make into a wooden stake.

Glowworms

We thought we could light our way with glowworms;
we were in the wrong place. My mother lit lanterns,
handed them round, the candles black with corpses.
We moved in single file, my father at the front but
hesitant, his hair in an anxious quiff. My mother said
go cheerfully and the ground will not open up.

She was wrong; at the end of the garden my twin fell
into a deep ditch, sat at the bottom in a dirge of muddy water,
laughed at us all crowded above.

I don't need your planks or butterfly nets she said
I can crawl.

She turned her back on us, went away from us,
her hands and knees sinking deeper;
still her voice sang out heroically
as the wind rattled the night.

The gerbil and the May Queen

My twin, in the form of the Queen of the May,
is riding in an open-top car. She's like a white wave
with red slashed through it, a child bride waving her cut flowers.
I am what happens to girls with fat knees and frog-coloured eyes –
Old Mother Hubbard, dancing in my brown dress and big men's
      boots!

But I am the one who will feel a tiny crunch in my slipper, later –
the cold fur, the still claws; the cage open, the chalky fall.
I will be the dead thing's little helper; with him
as he faces the telescoping burrow; with him
as he faces the shining whiskered face of god.

Lumbar puncture

I went to see my twin in her glass cubicle.
She had a bed whose sides went up and down
like a drawbridge. I looked at her in her glass castle
with all her notes and charts – she was a mathematical sum.

My twin had a needle in her spine.
I wanted to ask that needle what it saw
when it punched through her silvery skin,
what exactly it was doing there.

I sat on her bed in my deathly plain clothes
like an injured thing at the foot of a mountain.
I wanted us to go home to the stained glass
and the paper weights, to the bramble patch
where she would dare me to walk barefoot.
I even longed for her crutches and her paintings
of dead poets and her distorted shoes.

And was there a donkey? Was there a bear?
There were endless rows of glassed-in children,
ill and dying, nurses in their own clothes
with their cheerful wedding rings,
smoothing the patched-up sheets and pillows,
stroking the suddenly angelic heads.

The raft

I'm swimming out to the raft
in featureless conditions.
By day, white balance might be an issue
so I keep to the night time.
Everything's overexposed
the sky inky and filled with stars.

As I swim, unseen waves choke me,
my breath a damaged night moth that cannot land.
I'm somewhere between past and future
between through and over,
the buoys and the diving board a still life.

My father's standing back by the changing rooms
by the white buildings, in his shorts and soft shoes.
He's with my twin in her oversized buggy.
He's just given her a bag made of animal skin –
she is stroking it while her arms can still move.

Three Shires Head

Only we know this place – the meeting of three lands.
Wasps circle us; my father feeds them meat
to show us his love for them – we think my father
is a holy man, we sweep the dirt before him.
My mother is too busy knitting.

A stream flows under a wooden bridge.
My twin takes my arm, we clatter across like goats,
fearful that our hooves will give us away or lead us to horror.
We put our feet under the singing water; it's like a cure,
the stream passing over our numb skin.

My twin leans against me;
I want to hold her up and I want to step away,
watch her scrabbling in the shifting silver;
I know she will get up and walk one day.

Porch

God is giving us things; last night, our lost dog
appeared on our doorstep. Rain fell on the concrete porch.
She's the kind of dog you would wish for; ugly as sin,
with uneven eyes and a certain unkindness.

We keep her in the garage, curled in a deckchair.
We're at that age when we can only whisper
about these things, can only stroke each other
with casual accustomed pain.

Cliff

My father is further down the cliff face
held to the pale stone by fists of sea pinks.
He has no shoes on, his trouser legs flap
like badly pitched tents.

At the top of the cliff, my twin in her wheelchair
has twisted feet and her hands are curled
like sea horses; if only we could hear
the messages they hold.

There is no delight anymore, just the sweat
on my father's back and my twin's hair
cut with a bowl and wallpaper scissors –
the dark, glinting promise of it.

Typewriter

My twin moved to a downstairs room,
her handwriting unravelled – they bought
an electronic typewriter for her but still she
missed out letters. I watched her budgie's head
peeping out between the keys, our mother knitting up
my twin's dropped ball of words. We sang along
to *Tainted Love*, imitated the chatter
of the monkey muse.

No one knew her at that time, not even me.
She wheeled around her bed indomitably,
on her knee her muscular imagination spitting
and flexing. I stood behind her on my hated legs
pushed her forwards, ashamed of my head
which was a box of words scribbled on raffle tickets,
a glittering skull with glassy eyes like marbles
or counting beads.

We used to lie in our twin beds in our twin room
under heavy blankets, yellow nylon sheets
like a punishment. When we went to sleep
on an argument, my head filled up with twitching things.
I breathed in her stories, her intelligence –
her courage starved me.

Horse therapy

I watch my twin ride a horse
her arms still strong enough to be contrary.
She won't be led but canters round a barn
full of crippled teenagers she wants nothing to do with.
I sit at the edge on a fold-up chair grinding sawdust
under my unfashionable shoes, pulling at my short brown dress.
Suddenly, with a toss of her head, my twin gallops
out of the barn into another country.

Swallows turn to parakeets as she enters a forest
followed by flocks of children screaming *salud! salud!*
trying to touch her feet. Deeper in, her ears can still hear
jaguars roar as they devour the unclean. Her horse
could throw her but instead it chases butterflies
cut from the blue electric mountain –
if you press them to your face they smell of sulphur.

In a clearing women are frying fish, filling buckets
with pisco sour. They lift my twin down, make her crutches
from sticks, hand her a bucket in which she finds
my severed head. I have those ugly pigtails, that crooked fringe.
My twin decides to take me home, keep me in the compost heap
–

she wants my skull pure and clean, she wants its devotion.
She'll shrink it, hang it on the handle of her wheelchair,
its jaw opening and shutting, what it always says to her –
yes.

Motorbike

I draw the swirled blue curtains – here I am, sixteen,
midnight, midsummer, with Ian Curtis who's alive
and dancing on the blue linoleum ocean of our living-room floor.
I tell him it's all happening with Thomas, who calls himself
the ANTICHRIST yet calls a born-again evangelist for advice –
to touch or not to touch, that is our question.
The disciple wears a leather jacket in a hot room,
the smell of the chip shop downstairs makes me ill.
I sit on Thomas's knee looking at the Good News everywhere.

Through the arched window, I watch Roger the policeman
take my twin for a ride on his motorbike. He disregards
the great uncertainty of her limbs, her bare suggestible head.
Later, around the corner, he presses me to the wall.
He tells me she will die young, that her heart will stop
unless I agree to the laying-on of hands. Will it be his hands?
I've noticed how fat they are, tiny cherubic nails demonic with ink.

The Upper Room

I followed my twin as she followed god's ministers –
we worshipped their young men's bodies, their Stratocaster guitars.
When they sang *Jesus Loves You* – how we longed to be loved!
touched by the crucifixes dangling from their ears.

They promised my twin she would be reborn
in a different body. I came to see them carry her
in her long white dress into water, hold her under,
count under their pure suburban breath.

They were all there –
the policeman, the nun, the ones named Hawthorn;
they thought by carrying her in their arms upstairs
or on their motorbikes, they could give her back the gift
of motion – how wrong they were.

Once I pushed her downhill in her wheelchair so fast
I tipped her out onto stones which tore her poor feet,
feet she would not bind or straighten. Those Jesus boys
outdid each other with their thousand-watted prayers,
their faith taken by her as gospel, their attention to her
body taken as true.

Me they overlooked, even though I saw Christ
on Cheadle High Street barefoot in white flares.
I knew he would fill me by force with wilderness,
would always be there, would not cure me
but witness the counting down to breathlessness
the silent prayer –

give me death by water or lack of air
give me, at the window, not my father
but the three sacred hares.

My twin's child

Darling, don't go through the gate
or stumble into the lane looking for blackberries
or primroses – don't follow the gutter's rain-river
down to the sea. For now, be mine shiny as a lapwing
sharp sometimes with your cries like cut lemons.

Stay with me, let me take a magnifying glass to you
out of the sun – study your sweet smelling
elbows, the sturdy roots of your hair.
I'll know what you like, apples or chocolate,
custard or rice, what sleep does to you and joy.

I'll adore both your poppy and cornflower moods.
Everywhere you go there my face will be –
my eyes can't help falling on you even as I walk
with you into the garden. I'll be your boat, your blue fish,
your overcoat; I'll pack you with my scarves
when I find a way to leave.

I wish I was a mother – gentle, unyielding
keeping my fears under my tongue.
I wish we could live in a smuggler's cave
you and I, bravely with a view of the island.
We'd slip out onto the night ferry, Jack
I'd rock you to sleep to the gush and clank,
turn out the lights from the dockyard, sweet boy
I'd turn out the moon.

Birds

On the cardiac ward my twin lies twisted
on a high bed, a red circle on the wall behind
her head (danger of falling). She is attached
by a tube to a bag full of ravens who

sneak through the back of her hand
with their clever cruel birdness,
opening their wings like umbrellas
in her overcrowded chest. Canaries

flightless as steam irons, their nostrils
closed against the smell of blood,
are packed around her swollen heart
like explosives. They have been

wound round with fisherman's twine, held
underwater until their claws and beaks
are soft as rotten meat –
they cannot fight or speak. I find that I can

carry my twin in my arms, as they do
in the movies, past the nurse's station where
a caged, grey parrot says over and over –
birds not welcome birds not good.

Above the car park, a misplaced eagle studies us,
circles ruined buildings over psychiatry's
burnt-out shell. It watches me carry her
up a long stone staircase which ends in thin air;

she does not know where we are. I mean to step
with her across the threshold. My twin forces out words
on slow bubbles of breath, darkly –
I cannot say what they are.

Banished

Only my twin's new seven-foot circus-friend can speak to her.
He has the sinister neck of a clown, hands in giant gloves
he uses to put out her rage. They sit in her cave-room
stirring a cold fire of charcoaled shoes and condoms,
her crutches against the wall like snapped
branches.

I used to know her thinness in her green school jumper,
how to kneel to tie her laces, push her wheelchair into the sea.
Now she will not eat, not even the sweets I offer her –
I've rolled them in nostalgia's yellow powder, though
I know she cannot see. Maybe she'll feel them in the night
like a sandstone princess, slip them in her pockets
like innocent grenades.

I could have killed her just to have our room to myself.
Now her absence frets in corners. It makes no difference
if I wear a filthy mantilla over my gold mohican, on my feet
scuffed flamenco shoes, the path is always the same –
a dried-up riverbed, scrubby incantation of insects.
Even at the well, if I fill a bucket with water, the water
will be no good – my twin will see life in it, refuse to swallow.

One day there may be a congregation of visitors – my twin
will see them, stretch out her bones to greet them. I'll be
waiting outside on a steep brown horse, practising signs.
The succulents will be magnificent, our little sister a music-box
ballerina, roller-skating in tight circles on the furious ground.

Forbidden

When I kissed my twin's frozen forehead
I felt like chanting forbidden words, as we did once
not knowing their meaning, lying on the sofa
one head on each of its arms, a two-headed serpent.

Our mother was like a tree with an axe
through it – only one hand for each of us.
It didn't stop her smacking hard, hugging tight,
snapping elastic bands in our hair.
She wrenched our coats around us
as if by force she could make us loved.

We chewed over every story our mother told us –
with our matching teeth – I swallowed every word.

I wish now I could lower myself into my twin's
wicker box – it wouldn't matter would it if I crushed
her velvet dress? I could foetus myself within
her arms, determined she'd be more than me

again. I could curl up there like a little walnut
or a featherless bird. When they nailed us in
no one would remember how at the table
we shared chicken necks and livers

how we fought each other over wishbones.

Angels of Anarchy

The Oval Lady

What makes a woman a horse? The hyena knows. She herself has stolen my eyes – these are made of polished glass with lids of sand; I cannot cry. Instead, I am shaving the hair from my rocking horse, weaving it into my extravagant mane. I have been out in the garden with the scavenger, debating who most needs the spiny black shoes. She thinks she has the upper hoof because she has my breasts tied on but I always win. I know how to scoop out her heart with my first and fourth fingers. She is nothing but a stripy hysteric, carrying her vile smell around with her, screwing up her unkissable mouth. It's Daddy we need to beware of; I've seen him with flames in his hands, looking for us. If he wants to know my secrets he should look to the groves of hermaphrodite lime where a white horse leaps, a shining white mare with my fine pair of legs. She is perfectly executed with chalk sticks and spit. I go with her, beyond the gold and the cold terracotta; I'm a wild eye, then a pebble, a lost face, an egg.

After the painting 'Self Portrait' by Leonora Carrington

The Oneiroscopist

Afterwards, I like to sit on the pier between the sea and the not-sea and dry myself. If I had wings, I would spread them wide to feel the blood returning; pain has always brought me to life. What do I carry back with me? Bruised fruit, a scrap yard sphinx, guilt like the bloodied self. The nightmares I keep in a mermaid's purse where they scuttle about like a version of hell. I stab the clouds with my beak, cursing my lack of sight, fail to pierce the multitude of insects who talk about nothing but themselves. Down I go at dusk. It's like descending into a sea crammed with embryos, their uncanny eyes fixed on me as my diving suit loosens and billows. They slip inside, little ghoulish souvenirs, gasping, gasping. You'd think they believed that I'm the one who knows.

After the painting by Edith Rimmington

Frida's Letter

Mummy darling,

Here I am in the land of the gringo. The bears in Central Park are keeping me awake, eating fruit and slashing their paws. This morning I ate a small plate of Diego's shadow; he forgot to pin me inside his pocket and I'm in the blue house alone. My little 'any old monkey' has been crying quietly into my hair, there are two parrots under my skirts, joined at the heart. I've been speaking to my dead son or, at least, his broken body parts; he's given me his tiny bones to mend my shattered spine. He's making all this possible – sitting out of bed, leaning against walls in men's trousers, my head all flowers. On bad days, my feet become America, their rotten flesh like open mamey fruits, emerging like fleshy saints from a bed of coral. This could all be everything – he and I running into the flaming mountain. I know you think him degraded and toad-like, but he goes through me like a glittering pole, flying my birth flag. I rest in my dreams with him, where we are twined together with branches. He is my niño oscuro, Mummy, my niño precioso; we can't untangle the sheets when we meet, we can't disentangle our heads.

After the painting 'View of Central Park 1932' by Frida Kahlo

A Little Night Music

I held the golden flower's stalk in my hand; it was like touching nothing, like touching the core. I was wearing the doll's dress my mother made for my secret wedding with lust woven in, my hair swam up through the green light. My twin was shedding her dress like a sea snake, her child's polished body singing against the door-frame. She had put on a red shirt and wouldn't open her eyes, exhausted but ecstatic like a lost cygnet out on the water, a rag of sun in her hand. As for myself, every molecule had stopped. I looked to the opening door. I knew what I'd find there – a Christ in a caretaker's coat, waving us in; 'come quickly' he says, though we can barely stand, 'it's all over, even the door is touched by it can't you see it?' But we can't, we can't.

After the painting 'Eine Kleine Nacht Music' by Dorothea Tanning

House Containing Angel

You were shaken out of a new sheet into a doorway; three quarter light and a derelict floor. Not knowing how to behave you went up and down the broken staircase in your soft shoes and white stockings. Your knees were raw and red as a swine's mouth. A naked woman leaning over the banister offered you the opposite of suicide, blew softly on your wounds. Confused, you found yourself coming out of the wall like fungi or hanging from doorways. Your wings were blurred; you didn't know what to do with them or your whiteness, you were used to being underground, bandaged like a sick mole, mouth full of dirt and rusting. Now you hear seeds spilling out of the gutters and from the taps pours human hair. Everyone knows what you want – to lie down in Samuel Beckett's boat, your arms full of irises, an accordion playing and sunflowers bursting in the dust and glass that passes as air.

After photographs by Francesca Woodman

The Martello Tower

The Martello tower

You wouldn't recognise me, walled up
in my concrete cell, half-buried in these blue dunes.
My hair's as long as a cave woman's and I can't cut it –
I have no knife, nor key, just a slit window pierced
by sparse determined pines. There's nothing to do
but sit on this cool floor picking up handfuls of sand.
I choose the roughest grains, clench my fists –
make a strangled shrinking sound.

I live alone or with strangers. They come each dawn,
step from a boat made of shells, follow their burning shadows
to bring me rice and water. There are wise women. There are
men who arch their backs, drop cigarettes in the sand.
They are all lovers; their morning song dives into the ocean,
comes up like a bird shaking its green head. I would sing
with them but, the last time I saw my voice, it was yellow glass paper –
it made wounds where insects gathered.

You can see why they put me here, why they're glad
that I can't reach the men even if I wanted to,
or the women – even if I screamed I couldn't touch them.
They pull their boat out onto the sea with one or two gasps of water.

I've forgotten what another's skin smells like –
would it have little clouds of scent passing over it?
Would it taste of crabmeat or honey or like nails?
I think of us when we had only candles, a broken bed,
our hands like new tulips opening inside each other,
pushing backwards to the dark, red eye. We were so high,
so wild, the whole room collapsed around us, we were out
on a curved mountain, washed in a rush of river moss and stars.

I know you'll be twining your athlete's legs around another,
somewhere in an urban garden, your chest wheezing its little tune:
don't worry, don't even think of me –
I will not weep into my one cup of water.

Gay-Lyfe Pets and Aquatics

So we tie handkerchiefs round our faces
walk where nobody walks – along the Roman Road.
I notice the hard frost like white lichen
and lorries shaking the earth.

For three months I've been up all night,
swallowing bleach, trying to clean the dirt out of my mouth.

As we pass Pets and Aquatics, my friend gently pulls me in
saying – they're peaceful little souls; you should have some at home.

Out of the dim light their swollen eyes swim, their terrible lips.
At first it's a shock and I can only whisper their names

like a litany: tetras are strips of cruel rainbows
sooty black mollies shimmy on the stones
transparent glass catfish all heads and bones
soft water fish, hard water fish
the convict, the blue dolphin
white cloud mountain minnows.

I listen carefully when the man says
        'A small tank causes problems with internal organs';
I feel my liver and stomach, I massage my heart.
My friend nods wisely when the man says
        'I strongly advise a fishless cycle.'

Imagine washing gravel to the gravitas of Lieder!
I like the sound of *equalising* – to be soothed in a sack of warm water
before being freed.

But at the spawning tank I meet
the Egyptian Mouthbreeder, her mouth full of fry.
She's swimming in circles, chewing her babies alive, mouth jerking,
cheeks jumping, as if some devilish form was inside.

I fight my way through plaster bridges and plastic skulls
towards the narrow door, then out into a sharpness of rimey sun.

There's a green strangling springtime in my throat;
all I can think of are
             shoals of fish flipping
                      on my dirt-dry tongue
their little teeth piercing my cheeks like pearly-white fish-knives.

They didn't want to see me

They didn't want to see me until I had actually
stepped off the ladder, the bootlace's red loop
around my neck. Then, when little Glass-Hands
went for a cigarette, they gave me her bed,
threw me my rucksack emptied of plastic bags and pens,
glared at me with crazy sheepdog eyes.

I thought I would be laid down gently, that soft
white mice would run in and out of my mouth but, instead
they tied up my tongue. They were glad to see me
they said to each other, Nurse Cowheel, Nurse Hand-drill,
Nurse Retribution, Nurse Scrape, they said

this one likes to be restrained, held me humanely
one on each limb, twisting. The white line of sedation,
straight and unforgiving, took me speechless into every
howling monkey morning.

People came to see me. They seemed altered –
hot and unrecognisable in their flayed skin.
I might have loved them if I had not been cured of that.
I murdered them slowly one by one, felt love for their blood
which I painted the walls with, holding a paintbrush between my toes.

People came to speak to me. There was a girl
who threw herself from a motorway bridge, stopped
the traffic. She wheeled herself around the dayroom,
everyone admiring her crumpled legs.

Sometimes I longed for the sharp scratch of oblivion –
not to hear the night staff with their small vocabulary
ringing old school bells up and down the corridor

or the siren, as someone scaled the garden fence,
jumped down to where nurses were looking
at their phones and smoking.

Nurse Misogyny nailed my feet down, Nurse Fontanelle's
hands forced me to look straight ahead. The last thing I saw –
a suburban house opposite, a terrier behind the gate, sighing
and snivelling through its baby's teeth.

It was the dead princess on the TV who made us crazy –
we had been sitting around the walls, calmly clipping
and painting each other's nails, leaning forwards like
philosophers to smoke. Now the hair stood up on our backs
we were shocked into using ashtrays. The paparazzi cut
each other's wrists, burned each other's hands with cigarettes
just to steal a photo of her body entwined with briars,
the bloody pinpricks on her dress.

I knew who had done it – I had to tell. The brand-new nurses
not knowing of my genius, turned their backs and I was off
down an optimistic corridor to a cold stone step by an open door.
I found myself in a small off-stage replica of outside
could smell the incinerator and the lilac. The air was undecided,
hot then sharp as a meat cleaver, over-run with brambles
and bindweed. There were cameras everywhere. I stood
in a parallelogram of sun, longed to lie down on my side like
a huge black hairy sow. But I took a blade of glass, slashed forwards
through all the twisting and tangling. As the thorny cages opened
shapes and paths appeared to me, flowers fell on my head
like paranoia's cure.

Then, out of a dark corner, nurses came towards me like tanks
screaming *get back to your bed*. I felt again that woman in the night
climbing on top of me like a farm-dog, dragging up my nightdress,
her hot cheek against mine, her hand which smelt of mashed potato
crushing my mouth. Her weight on me was like a cow's. I knew
all about cows – I pushed my fingers into her eyes and twisted
her eyeballs like lychees. She could not object – I was kissing her
so hard her lips filled up with blue blood. I could see the two of us
on screen after screen, fighting for life, framed by honeysuckle.

Wincobank

All you could imagine you deserved – the gas towers rising and falling,
the promise of their frostbitten, scaffolded hearts.

You told me you could not write. Pylons stamped across the page,
snow-light crept around your jagged edges.

There was a phone box you liked to shut yourself up in, a scuffed
blue path at the edge of the terraces you tightrope-walked along.

In Wincobank in winter the buses stopped halfway up the hill,
they could not reach you. There was nowhere to go –

no money for the corner shop where people chatted in their severed
dog-head slippers, no entry at Shire Green Working Men's Club.

You told me you longed to go back to your home made of plastic sheeting
and branches, pieces of string, where in the mornings, rain would pool

at the threshold. You would stretch out your tongue like a giraffe and drink.
I liked to think of muddy water filling up your stomach with water boatmen

and scum. The fire could not be lit, the town was barricaded against you,
local women spat on your breasts.

When you described to me the night a lightless car drew up and men
dressed as militia threw a stinking wave of maggots over you –

did you expect my pity? How you loved to be persecuted! You rubbed
wood ash into your skin, ate seaweed, raised the ghost of Janis Joplin.

How solid the house was, like a meat freezer; pigs as bloody
as Friday night dresses hung on a rack. Naked

except for the stars shaved into your head, you climbed
inside a carcass, your face peering out from its pink lace neck.

If there had been anyone there, they would have said it suited you;
that you had found your place.

You brought with you young Americans, armed and metallic
as grain towers, who filled the yard with the decomposing sun,

their foul-smelling, incomplete bodies, their broken jaws
and carved-up faces pressed against the window.

I expect the gas fire sputtered, lost its blue –
a cigarette held against it only smoked. You feared the body

shape painted on the yard's glass-topped wall, the cats
who broke in like urine-scented storm troopers pissed on your feet.

Of course you had no one to wash them; I was not the only one
who refused.

You told me how you crouched in an army-surplus sleeping bag
on a rented sofa, like a piece of origami, watching snow fall.

Taraloka

I'm stalked by bulrushes
do goldfinches live in burrows?

is a pond still a pond
even if a straight line?

I've seen goldcrests fly through a locked door
dragging coils of wild garlic

plovers dive-bomb my very clothed body
the dawn chorus all owls

I remember her untouchable hands
their harshness when she opened them

released me too soon

Can I fight the darkness that holds me together
with delphiniums

stand on a bridge
a startling of swallows like jacks-in-a-box

shouldn't it all end now?

It's heaven down here, my blue boots
stepping out into the wooden presence

of wheatear and nightjar –
the longing of my face

to be underneath the peat bog
the frog-like stink of loss

Behind my sister's house

Blue dog jumping snaps up time.
I myself no longer move except when shoved
by this swan-like presence, which is both
above the clouds and here beside me
crushing my lungs with its brick-like wings.
It keeps needling me with coincidence, pushes me
to the little copse below the motorway
bluebells buried under foam snow – an accidental sofa.
It steps out from behind a hawthorn in full flood
calls me a prisoner in a waterless pit. It starts to rain.
I kneel in the stupid grass, can't bring myself to drink.
I will do what I'm told – delete myself.

Searching

(after Jack Gilbert)

I find that darkness has no red in it –
little distorted animals are marching round my bed
showing their blue tongues
making their subdued symphonic sounds.
They've left their eggs and sticks outside
my window where a wolf is splitting sticks
between its teeth to start a fire.

Take me out to the hunters and waders!
Out to the acid spill of stars – my teeth clatter
like nails against this milky glass. The animals
press their eyelids shut, fill my eyes with sparks.
At the foot of my bed, old dog is turning his ears
in all directions, turning back to eat his own skin.

Foundations

Another carnivorous day without story or shining;
in the cellar mushrooms greet you, deathly white
and vanishing. You take down a splintered board,
climb into musty foundations. The gap is small –
in a concrete tunnel, you crawl like a soldier, everywhere
strange ecstatic light, the smell of hawthorn. Time

lurches forwards. You emerge into sudden darkness,
a severe rehearsal for the time you will not save yourself
but shrink like an old woman, bent forwards,
studying cigarette-butt mountains, the hostility of linoleum.
You'll be guarded by goat-ghosts who bite at your scars.

Do not think of yourself as alive. Instead,
dream of sisters gathering in the garden, tall
and straight as lampposts, fuchsia lips, headlight eyes.
They wear boiler suits, thick gloves, are moody
and hard-hearted in their brilliance;
sleep will come only with the shriek of falling water

Babysitting

I knew I wasn't old enough – I told them their baby
would fall from the bed, scream until I picked her up,
planted her in the aquarium where she could wave her arms
forever, like coral. Bubbles of crimson screams would rise
to the surface, to disappear like relatives from around a body.

Her father was a short man in black bowtie and patent shoes.
When his wife went up to find the baby, he licked my
knees free of gravel, swallowed eighty sharp grey stones.
He said when they opened him up they'd find nothing sharp
just five little goatlets, woolly and indignant.

I'd wrapped their little boys tightly in striped sheets
and old grey blankets, like our mother did when she tucked us in.
I longed to be held in place then by love's restraint.
Now, held down by five grown men, a sixth with a needle
I think of goats and pigs and wolves –

I choose wolf
I am wolf –
I huff and I puff and I blow them all sky high.

Coal bunker

A cry comes again from the coal bunker;
I'm on the sledgeable, tar-papered roof,
scrape my palms raw as I slither down.
Patches of snow on the ground;
a single snowdrop staring as I kick the door shut.

In the house –the larder.
In the larder – the meat safe.
In the meat safe – the poison.

Up the stepping stone path to the snicket
I go. I've lined up the dolls (no blindfolds) –
I don't know which one I'll start with but I have
my brother's gun nestling in its holster like a foetus.

I'll take them over the edge – they've always
wanted to go. I promise I've tried the gun out –
discovered something homely about its smoky metal soul,
the way my mouth shrinks to fit its snout.

Poor dolls! They think they will be saved.
They need to understand: all there will be
is a white plain, a white sky, not a speck of dust
or vegetation. No, not even the sound of birds
scraping insects from branches.

Megan McMorran

At Megan McMorran's they have a glass porch
where waxy begonias suffer and die. Her mother
is out, her father so absent he doesn't even have
a name. We drink from the second-hand sideboard
to our adulthood to come.

Upstairs, in her mother's room – the smell
of the Avon Lady, a rosary I do not recognise
or know how to use; a glass-backed hairbrush,
a triptych mirror, a dressing table with a swivelling
stool. I sit and look at myself. I am a spaniel
with slightly greasy fur. Suddenly

there is a movement in the mirror; a man
lurches forwards like a falling tree. My scream
does not have time to shape itself. I turn. No one
is there. Except Megan McMorran, lounging on the bed,
looking at porn she has found in a suitcase. She glances up:
don't worry she says, *he looks but doesn't touch.*
There is all this white stuff in the air.

Bungalow

They put up special wallpaper: hand-painted rose buds which, on our first night, swallow us.

Spat out, we sit at Granddad's feet. He walks around us in his dairyman's shoes.

Pink crocheted lady over the toilet roll, smell of strange soap.

In his garden, potato trenches you can crawl into, the unbelievable taste of tayberries.

Behind his bus driver's back we dig his fuchsia bushes up with bare hands.

Seaweed hangs in the doorway predicting hurricanes, plagues of brittle ladybirds.

The Old People die of Nanny's bread and butter, her inedible jam tarts, her tea trolley.

Too many clocks, lighted cigarettes, yawning rabbits made of cabbage leaves.

Five children in a tiny red sitting room – I don't know why their electric fire doesn't turn us back to ash.

Well dressing

My mother and I are dressing
a dry well with violets and sorrel –
not the flowers themselves
but the spirit of the flowers.

Sky is coming in, going out
as cruel as the lake we scuff across.
Ground is thick with frogs –
how they sigh and crinkle.

My mother wears black satin
her feet bound with frayed lace.
His face, she keeps saying,
when he did it, his triumphant face.

When I wake, she is fanning my face
with a new fern, holding out the last bag
of water, as if to a horse.
I will go soon, with no shoes.

Let there be walls and no windows
a sack to sleep in on the cool impersonal earth.
I have always longed for a pitcher
and a prayer mat – days and nights of verse!

My father in the monastery

Lauds

His bare feet at 5 a.m. make him unsteady.
An ashen wind scoots under the door. He hears
the grass laughing under its snow-dome, dresses
angrily in the brown dress, thinks *my stomach
is an empty whale*. The rope around his waist
pulls him back to himself. A pigeon sits
at the glassless window, swollen to fit it like bread.

Sext

There is the walk along the vast corridor
and no seat. There is the walk through the blue
garden where two fat ducks are grazing like small
brown sheep. He enters the hall as the bell is about
to ring. Brothers are swimming in the yellow river.
He cannot sing the psalms. He is not speaking to Christ.

But there is the eating which calms him.
There is the breathing which strengthens him.
There is obedience which listens to him.

Vespers

He is painting icons with a brush like a needle.
Candles spit like camels. The monks regard him
from the corner of their eyes; they have seen
him before. They know he longs to paper
the walls with questionable books. They know
he is not afraid of their questions.

Compline

He stands in the snow to view the moon
through a telescope. The cold is a crawling insect
within his blood. At his feet, a dove like a fallen moon
which sees in all directions. He kneels and lifts it
to his chest, feels its tiny lungs rise and fall –
an echo, a mirror, an encouragement.
He does not need to bow his head.
Silence is blanketing his naked feet.

Conversation at Cricieth Castle

The point says my father is that my legs are like curtain poles
my chest is a shoebox filling with glue.
When I walk I clank and rattle like an old cart.

Great seascape he adds turning his back to the ruins
but colour would add something – did I mention the planks of wood
pinned to my sides?

Imagine us both in the garden, Daddy,
having leapt from the sofa to the great outdoors.
I would find you among the dog roses and mare's tails.
You'd be colouring the anaemic daisies in, humming.

The point, I say is that I need to go back to the time
I could ride on your shoulders and turn you
turn you into the sun.

Behind my father a signpost says don't climb on the...
I can think of nothing to do but pull my coat around me
imagine blossom falling from the monkey puzzle tree.

Subsongs

It was like shaking a baby or beating a rug
or walking in on myself having appalling sex in a basement,
an enormous cat trapped outside between the window and the wall.
I was reminded of that woman who smelt of stale Frascati
and aftershave – like Blanche she kept the lights out,
spent the whole night quoting Dorothy Parker.
I don't know why I was lying in her twisted grey sheets
avoiding contact with her skin except that my heart
was broken and unbearably meaty.

After the hurricane I was a fallen tree. I stole eggs
from devastated nests, compared their size and shape,
threw them down my throat where they lodged like
pale blue tumours. I could have died like this –
first the drying out, then starvation, then birds shortening
their songs before they split like axed wood. The noise
they made not music but high-pitched abbreviated pain.

I remember when I hit my father he was well.
We were walking on Plymouth Hoe in winter.
I was mad as salt flats, accused every man of rape.
Now he's attached umbilically to his oxygen machine
which inhales and exhales in the corner. I touch his sharp knee.
He tells me in his dream he's sitting on a pile of bones
for which he's responsible – he wants to take them to join his father
who was buried at sea. It's too far. Even if he rode a horse
into the icy waves, its hooves thick with frost, his horse would
fall away like a building. Even my father can't walk on water.

Anchoress

After rolling downhill with me in a blood-stained carpet,
after brushing red clots of snow from my coat,
after weaving a path through the frozen marshland,
my father left me in a clearing, alone. He said
he was going to put a gun to his stomach
at the shrine of our lady of mortal sin,
that he wanted the long silhouette of a drawn-out death,
that he wanted the actual pain.

My father left me his knapsack the colour of lichen,
no food inside or maps or water, just handfuls
of mist and ferns unfurling. He gave me a vision
of my coming into being – I was in Christ's body
clinging to his heart. Something had gone through me
something clean and beautiful, I rocked like
a cracked egg.

I had a vision of my coming into time –
late spring, heaps of blossom in the garden,
wagtails stuffing their beaks with straw.
I heard Christ say 'what will I do with them, the mothers
beating their children, the fathers exercising their guns?'
It was me who heaved myself from the wound in his side
held open the rent muscle, the haemorrhage of veins.
I wrapped my soul around me like a second skin –
I could pick bits from me, flutter them into the void.

My father's field glasses

out of their soft-lined case, they hung on his chest
like an extra black heart. They gave us a world
of ruined cattle, shining paths like rivers, shining rivers
like paths. I studied my big sister down at the stream
searching for blue john, quartz, fool's gold – anything
my father put a name to; the thrill of him moving the world
in and out of focus with his hands.

out of my new window, brave city birds in their little theatre
of wilderness. I lift my father's field glasses, witness
the blackbird's silent beak opening, closing;
behind its rivet eye – what?

the tiny blue and yellows fluff themselves in a bare tree
plunge down to drink the sun with finches gold and green.
For a moment I lose sight of them as steam from the laundry rises,
covers everything.

once I saw my father spy a stream of deer, red on the opposite
hillside – the joyous speck behind them our keen-eyed dog.
We all ran wailing come back, come back but she couldn't hear.
Now I put my nose to the red-lined case and breathe
leather, sheep's jaws, heart's blood, old dust.

Landing, Plymouth Rock

Susannah White, passenger

There were no cabins –
we squatted below deck with the livestock.
Geese burst against the steep ship's sides –
sacks of guts and feathers.

As we dragged our skirts ashore, I thought
we would be in our proper element.
But the sand shifts in waves and fills our eyes.
The wood we brought is swollen, the nails rusty.
In the wind there's a new silence.

The men have gone to search for food –
it's Lizzie and Mary and I together.
We have fashioned a shelter
from bent-knuckled branches and blankets.
We skin and eat an injured gull.

Mary bellows and bleats as her child tries
to come. All night we sing to her
songs of the forest and meadow.
At daybreak we pull him out, hope lost.
She holds him up, crying *what am I to do with this?*

This life is a gradual narrowing of light.
Why give her an empty vessel
with twisted limbs and shut eyes?
She cannot even bury him –
the sand covers, uncovers.

Lizzie and I hide him with rocks, carefully but still the stones still kick his skin. We do not place a cross. When Mary sleeps, Lizzie and I hold our babies to us – dear Oceanus, my darling Peregrine.

Thomas White, who dyed of the general sickness

They tell me I am lying on a beach in daylight. I must be looking up because everything is blue and spacious but underneath me the sand is corpse and carrion cold. When I move my head from side to side it makes a mean little scratching sound. My hands and feet are the size of ships. I miss the dark afternoons already, though I see they have invaded my skin. The flesh crawls out of my mouth which will never now be kissed. My wife prays for me, at a distance, turning the baby's face away. I hear her singing rock-a-bye-baby. I am on that tree top. I would sing to him also if my lungs were not sodden paper. *Mummy make the clouds keep still* – the way they rush over me makes me despair. Are they going home? I could go with them in a cooking pot or cradle, I would kiss the barren field, Susannah, I would bless the scabbed apples, the potato blight. Oh for stunted pumpkins still bright on the white earth! My arms like the trees here reach in one direction. *Daddy make the wind stop* – it will kill me with its whipping and wailing. Will Susannah bring me a sponge full of water, a sea biscuit? By dark I will become November, raising my purple cloak, snuffing myself out.

William Bradford, Elder

They say her eyes were defiant, as though she willed it;
saw ten rosy crabs on the ocean floor and yes
wanted to be there, weaving little boxes out of seaweed,
naked and hairless, a girl-shaped gap in the water.

She cannot tell me a thing, her teeth rigid, her lips
white as cuttlefish. I close her mouth gently with a bruised
sponge, lift her head, heavy as a tomb boulder, comb wet spasms
from her hair. When her shadow tipped over, when her dress
filled up with sullen waves, who, with their life,
should have saved her?

Once, I followed her muddy tracks to the meadow,
a flock of hens flew against my legs in bursts. It was summer
too early, the bluebells shocked. I came across her
sitting in the shimmering grass, covered in daisies. Sparrows
were fluttering at the back of her neck. She let me lie on her then,
clothed and desperate, my hands tied behind me like a robber.

Now, I am looking at an imaginary fish a boy has brought me –
it is the shape of a half-closed eye, its scales have just stopped clacking.
Christ, this is when you are needed; when a fractured moon falls
between dune and sky, I have a drowned wife, men with green wounds,
not an ear of wheat anywhere.

The Longest Journey I

(after the painting by Ana Maria Pacheco)

I thought I would be alone with Him,
wearing my all-in-one
green satin,
my sensible canvas pumps.
I expected to have oranges and
a notebook for the journey.

The shock of my almost
nakedness makes my knees
tremble like a kicked table;
someone has dressed me in a
striped tankini –
my needle heels stick in the planking,
the weight of my stomach makes us list
                    South.

Our little vessel won't be breaking much
ice –
it is barely He-worthy.
Poor souls, cowering, only one
with a fish; the wet sail
slapping us blue.

I think that is a woman
next to me, gas-masked.
Her candle is as thin as her dribbling thigh.
She says *we are many, aren't we,*
us sharp-teethed creatures?
and holds the man next to me by his
                    sex.

71

Trefeglwys

(for Janice)

No letters come or parcels tied with mildewed string –
only a lamb, mewing at the back door, sodden and trailing
an old placenta. We take down a cleaver, make the animal
free. Entranced, although we have nothing to feed it on, it dances
in the kitchen until nightfall when hail like buckets of rice
is thrown against our windows.

We don't sleep, although we are sick to the stomach
of amphetamines and cribbage and blind man's buff.
Once we had fireworks in a bucket of sand. We had visions
then and musical instruments – we actually chose candlelight.
By morning there was always a body of ice
on the inside of our windows.

Nobody cries
we gave that up long ago.

Truck driver, 1983

He is like a man I met in the 80s who,
in the high hot cab of his truck, put his hands
under my shirt, spoke to my naked breasts as though
they were his children. Then he went back to his driving.
The rain and dark polished the windscreen,
I saw no lights or stars or even hedges –
the world had become water. I swam in my shapeless
feminist clothes, took off my shirt to make a float for him.
His steel toe caps dragged him down. I knew
I could dive down and take off his boots, tenderly
pulling his laces with my teeth. But I wanted to see his hair
floating on the water like something forbidden, the water
close over him like a mouth. I did not want him to suffer.
I wanted his hands to be clean, unfatherly, so that
I could feel his warm transgression again.

Gap year

It was better back in the old country
before we lived above the barbers' shop –
a room with a toilet in one corner, clouds
of parakeets chattering greenly above the square.
Crowds of lost tourists drink insanely beneath
our window; a few foreign armies throw their
weapons down to scratch and swear.

How I long to take you to the outskirts
where the anarchists live – I'd sell
my guitar to the Catalan on the corner,
give up beer. When we arrived
no one would be there to greet us –

there'd be no road blocks or razor wire
we'd step right across the line between street
and garden. You'd be impressed by my reticence –
I wouldn't kiss you, though you begged me
I'd read you translations from the guidebook
pull softly at the lobes of your ears.

Severe weather warning

Something shakes you awake:
not light, longing for the dry side of your window,
not horses below like paintings of horses,
not stump-legged ponies or the swilling of sewery water;
no – it is her, standing in the doorway
her hair all crumpled, with reeds twined in it,
her shoes like warped suitcases
her dress soaked and tied with a rope.

She says *I think they may have gone*
taking our compass, our biscuits and our vase
of clean water. She tells you she saw your friend
(the one who gave you that tattoo)
floating down the street face up,
turning and turning like a stick on the flood.
The water kept sliding over his face;
she says she ran like a goat, she swam out
to greet him, but his glassy eyes said it was
useless, all useless.

Here she is with nothing to give you
but the story of it, her dreams of worms
and ex-lovers, a wreath of plastic flowers
she has washed and washed for you.

Seamstress's notebook

The rhythm of my foot stitching. Across the filthy road
a dog fight; men stark against the light throw

bricks and when the beasts part, beat them with sticks
as if they were capable of music.

I'm thinking about the piano my father never learnt
and I've put away the half-sewn garment

he'll never wear. I might have sewn
insects or a coded message or rose hips into its hem.

Oswald Road

I've retreated like a deer into the wood
I've lain down in leaves, making little huffs of hot breath in air.

You will not follow me out of love
or curiosity, but out of bitterness.

I'm tired of climbing down into the earth, lighting lamps.
Let me kneel under the frosted moon and want to live.

I'm making piles of steps taken on the final slope of the mountain,
they shift in the wind – will they blow the door open?

Dreams of warthogs

I am one of those bad girls who converses
with dirt, snuffling in the shrubbery.
I do the same thing over and over.
I am pricking out seeds, weighed down
by summer's gaping terror. I am
cultivating a horror of blue hydrangeas.

I find myself asleep in a blue room,
a corpse decomposing in my attic,
a spade gleaming in my luminous yard.
I am selling all my clothes
in underground tunnels, becoming
naked and thin in a roar of stale air.

I once lived with warthogs in a dark hut
and pissed outside in the cloud forest's
steam where the idle paparazzi flashed
like glowworms. Drove my father's car
through tangles of snakes, the florescence
of spiders floundering on vinyl seats.

I was a bad child with rage bent backwards.
I am an empty pram. I am walking uphill,
over and over, through damp clouds descending,
past heartless rocks that cough and creak,
the blow and hiss of the distant sea. And overhead,
swarms of oystercatchers are sharpening their beaks.

The Boatshed Café

These are your first instructions:
never look each other in the face
or put your fingertips together
like a church. In the Boatshed Café
we will be watching you
and the red walls will remain red.

Out on the veranda
you will want to smoke but *you are not to smoke*,
or drop your rubbish in the eely water –
remember, the tide comes into your doorstep.
We know the time you climb through the glass wall
everyday, into bed. We will observe you
waiting for the mud to disappear,
for the sunset's invasion.

We also listen to the radio, especially the weather.
We know about your feet which are swollen
with the rain. Your eyes have a leafy tinge.
Don't be tempted to take him to the mangrove swamp
we are already there, underneath the duckboards,
keeping our eyes open.
Don't think about *that part of him*
or stand with your thighs in that position;
we can hear you clip clop clip clop
over the wooden pathway
saying to him *no one will find us here, no one.*

Jesus on a train from Mumbai

I was dragged from the train by English tourists, as the tall man
from Tamil Nadu called 'coffee coffee' in his soft sad voice.

They had been to too many temples, mistaken the pigeon-feeding ritual
for a message from god. All they wanted was for me to sing songs

altered by death but when I opened my mouth I vomited water hyacinth –
they beat me with metal rods from London buses, whilst the schoolboy bird

whistled outside. Women wrapped in blankets came to view me,
carrying boulders on their heads to mend the roads. When they judged me

bloody enough, we went for chai at a shack by the roadside,
a statue of St George in a glass case spoke. There was mist and no view.

In damp fields, men sold bags of candyfloss to over-dressed newly-weds,
heaps of carrots, sickening as goldfish. Children followed us like skinny dogs,

their ribs rotten as railway tracks. In the back yard of his brother's house
a man invited us into his concrete hut, model trains mounted on the walls

like something shot. His brain was smaller than a mouse's.
He showed us a dead kingfisher the size of a rat, its enormous

beak open, about to speak, asked me to bless it.
I could not. I had shared a bed with my mother, under the same

mosquito net, had watched my father miraculously pleasure
thirteen women with his thirteen hands.

Woodcutter

I had sent the children out early for mushrooms,
I can describe them to you exactly;
she was wearing her brown wool dress
and her red coat; her hands were white with edelweiss.

I don't remember his clothes (who remembers
a boy's clothes?) He was as tall as I am, brilliant
with an axe and a chisel. That was my hand
guiding his, the wooden handle curved to our fist.

She had set out my food – dry cheese and fruit cake,
three litres of wine. She was crazy as a mountain rat,
always tipping water on the fire, crying all night
for her peg doll's lost souls.

I trust the forest like the palm of my hand,
but not the burnt out trees, the funnels of snow.
Not the frozen lake, drawing them onwards,
to feel the blue air burn their lips and their lashes.

Now, I step outside to bring in the washing –
the shirts are chittering with hoarfrost;
this one's the good thief, who snaps in my hands,
this is the other, throwing white arms around me.

I tell you I am glad at the crack and rustle of it,
how it smothers my chapped lips –
how it loves me!

Grandmother

My grandmother's shoes are laced-up tight
beneath her dress of stretched violet.
Her jars of beans are counted and polished
her starched bleached sheets hung out to dry.

Streuth, girl she says, when a man beats you
it's with the beam of love in his eye.
I'll choose for you a man made of meat –
if he feeds you, he'll feed you the best cuts of the beast.

Here come the men like a full river
here the men come like a rope, thrown.
They bring their gifts of broken-legged horses
ready-made cigarettes and pressure pans.

They talk to Grandmother in her breathless kitchen
as she skims the cream or stirs the tub.
They talk to Grandmother in the ticking parlour
where she rocks and rocks a creaking pram.

If they put their knuckles or flesh against me
I'll kick the parlour chairs, I'll break their hands.
You can shut me up in the oasthouse, Grandmother
my neck will be snow-smirred, scalded with ice.

I may be gloved and small-footed, Grandma,
I may seem in my black dress all shy of the plough –
but my empty bowl gleams like a chosen thing
and my heart, Grandma, my heart is a field.

The nameless tree

I used to know my name when it was presence.
In our little copse we would watch our acorns
plummet down, singing their freedom songs.
Now my catastrophic brothers have been felled,
sawn into body parts. No more shaking off our
secret letters, no more children

crouching in the hedgerows like ground birds,
or horses pinned to the hillside like flies
or sheep stapled beside them or tiny stones
on the ground with shadows like black teeth.

Children used to know the importance of plovers,
their glove-like wings. They could recite the rules
of the Underworld, the need to curse like men.
I would hear their hearts beating as they crept out
into steaming sun, into light which fell on brambles
and burst like seed pods.

Now, they'd have to come by boat –
our meadow is flooded and barren. Sometimes
through my watery eyeglasses, I see myself reflected.
What is left to me is trench foot, buttercups and praying
for the wisdom to live in this colour grey sameness.

Hatch

They could've told me I'd live to see
the stoning of my husband in broad daylight
(every brick, every paving stone)
and him in his best white frock.

I'd walked out at twilight to bring him home
not minding him being late, not caring
that he had his own living room –
a hatch was all I needed, a window
onto his dogskin rugs, his little metal men.
I lived for the times when things passed between us –
plates of onions, clothing, school reports, pliers,
light bulbs, chess boards, jugs of hot water.

At other times I would sit on the carpet
my small chin raised
clasping my ill-looking children.

The men were always jealous of the squeak
of seafood between my husband's teeth,
teeth that were chiselled by the upper ranks of angels
who sculpted also his beatific backside.
Women would pray to touch his calves, so shapely
he couldn't walk without them caressing like lovers.

My husband could have died at home, clutching a clean
handkerchief, a letter of apology in his ragged trouser pocket.
I would have read that letter, burnt it and
as usual, in states of emergency,
lit the blue camping stove with his elongated matches
started the tea.

States of happiness

I was like something made out of wood, ankles buried in the new lawn, ash tree arms rocking. My hair grew at a strange angle. I held my mother's babies one after another, cleaned their filthy heads. We drew a curtain across my father who was like a gift promised by mistake. I dressed as a gypsy often, felt sure I had a caravan somewhere. When the rag and bone man called I longed to leave, I envied the horse its blinkers. From my father I learnt the art of brooding – no one could love me, I was not of that mind.

The day the bleeding started I fell in love twice. There was the girl who hid with me in long grass behind her house, whose kiss was beautifully carved, who held me shyly with her pastry-coloured legs. The boy had football boots that flashed like sunburnt doves. When we passed his whole body blushed. His blundering kisses were fuelled by gin, he put his heavy hands on me. Who was more frightened? Him, stranded on my bed or me, forcing my hands into cacti on the stairs, falling into the garden where a fuchsia hedge bled on the paving and the sky was delightfully red.

I managed four strange years before I bore a baby like a yellow fish. The midwives woke me with their metal hands, their words as dark and squat as woodstoves. They told me, *say goodbye to your ghost baby, she hangs like a bird in the sky. Remember there are at least four states of happiness – you'll climb the ladder and find one when it's time.*

After April

(for Bronwen)

when I go back   if I ever go back
   will a branch fall from the tree I lie under
      suddenly   like a sword or a wand
                    each shadow the same

awake all last night   almost cremated
   by hospital bedding   hospital heat
      my window opens only enough to let dawn in
               an urgent blackbird comes shockingly to life

will I hear it again ever   perfect pitch in a dead tree
   walk through cumuli of mayflower   magnolia   white halo
      of butterflies   crack willow
               where jackdaws strut with sticks
     and moss   the shaggy fox plucks a rabbit up
               shakes it free of its side-eyed life

when I go back   if I ever go back
   will my twin and I play again at the crease
      watching my father walk in to bat
          will a red stitched ball land in dry soil   long grass
  a thrush rattle her panic   like a snake

if I meet them at the boundary   all my dead beloved
  will we go back   to perfect possibility
     a clutch of souls caught   together
            speckled treasure   in a nest of gorse.